The Chooky Brae

The first play in D. C. Jackson's 'Stewarton Trilogy' for
Borderline Theatre Company, *The Wall*, won the Best
Ensemble at the 2007–8 Critics' Awards for Theatre in
Scotland and was shortlisted for the Saltire Society/Royal
Mail Scottish First Book of the Year Award. It was
followed by *The Ducky* in 2009. *The Chooky Brae*
completes the trilogy in 2010. *My Romantic History* was
staged earlier in the same year by the Bush Theatre and
Sheffield Crucible. He has also had short plays produced
by Oran Mor (*Matinee Idle*, *Drawing Bored*, *Out on
the Wing* and *Company Policy*) and the Arches Theatre
Company (*Hello*, part of *Spend a Penny*). He is working
on new plays for BBC Radio 4, the National Theatre of
Scotland and the Royal Court, and was the Pearson
Writer in Residence at the Royal Court for 2008.

D. C. JACKSON

The Chooky Brae

faber and faber

First published in 2010
by Faber and Faber Ltd
74–77 Great Russell Street
London WC1B 3DA

Typeset by Country Setting, Kingsdown, Kent CT14 8ES
Printed in England by CPI Antony Rowe, Chippenham, Wiltshire

A CIP record for this book
is available from the British Library

ISBN 978-0-571-27431-4

2 4 6 8 10 9 7 5 3 1

This trilogy of plays is dedicated to Eddie Jackson.
I couldn't possibly have a better father or producer.
I owe him everything.

Acknowledgements

I wrote the first draft of this play at the Hotel Chevillon in Grez sur Loing, France, where I was staying as the beneficiary of a Robert Louis Stevenson Fellowship award. Huge thanks are due to Fiona Graham and everyone else who facilitated that. Also I owe a debt to Kirsty Williams for all her help, which went above and beyond what could be thought reasonable, and Kenny Miller – a fantastic collaborator and a wonderful man. As ever – thank you Liz Lochhead, Ben, Edward and Jacqueline Jackson, Steve King, Dinah Wood and Lisa Foster.

The Chooky Brae was commissioned and produced by Borderline Theatre Company, Irvine, and first performed at the Palace Theatre, Kilmarnock on 2 September 2010. The cast was as follows:

Gordon Gordon Stewart Porter
Irene Gordon Anita Vettesse
Norma Sally Reid
Barry Scott Hoatson
Rab Jordan Young

Director Kenny Miller
Designer Neil Haynes
Lighting Designer Graham Sutherland
Stage Manager Fran Craig
Deputy Stage Manager Kirsty Airlie
Deputy Stage Manager Suzie Goldberg
Wardrobe Supervisor Jennie Loof
Producer Eddie Jackson

Characters

Gordon Gordon

Irene Gordon
his estranged wife

Barry Gordon
their son, twenty-two

Norma Gordon
their daughter, eighteen

Rab McGuire

THE CHOOKY BRAE

The Scene

The former council house in Stewarton the Gordons bought in the late 1980s and have lived in ever since. It is Christmas and the small, neat living area is appropriately festively decorated. A tree in the corner of the room has presents underneath. Two doors lead off – one, stage right, to the kitchen (off), the other on the back wall to the hall (off). Stage left of the sitting room, divided by a wall, is a small room with a toilet, a sink and not much else, accessed from the hall (off).

Act One

*Lights up on the Gordon family home. Gordon Gordon
sits in the middle of the lounge in a wheelchair. He is fifty
and has recently returned to live with his estranged wife
and children after suffering a stroke. Barry Gordon is
twenty-two, he lies prostrate on the couch in his pyjamas.
Gordon has a small box on his lap which he opens. He
produces a king-sized cigarette paper and begins the
laborious process of rolling a joint using only his right
hand.*

*Barry glances over at him briefly before he returns to
his masterful inactivity. Gordon toils on valiantly and
eventually has the tobacco and marijuana inside the
paper. He fashions a roach from a Christmas card and
eventually manages to lick and close the joint. It isn't a
thing of beauty but it is functional. He puts it in his
mouth and begins to search for his lighter. He realises it is
sitting on the coffee table, just out of his grasp. He looks
over at Barry then takes the joint out his mouth and
appeals to his son for aid –*

Gordon Gordon L-l-l-l-lighter.

Barry ignores him.

L-l-l-l-lighter.

He continues to ignore him.

Lighter. F-f-f-f-fugging. Lighter.

Barry Gordon I'm sorry?

Gordon Gordon L-l-l-l-lighter. P-p-p-path me tha fu-fu-
fugging l-l-l-l-lighter.

*Barry sighs and gets up to get the lighter for him.
Gordon places the joint back in his mouth in
anticipation. Barry hands him the lighter and then,
just after, plucks the joint out of Gordon's mouth. He
quickly takes a couple of steps back so he is out of his
father's reach. Gordon swings at him like King Kong
with his right arm.*

Fugg off. Fugg off. G-g-g-g-gisme tha back.

Barry Gordon What would Mum say? You've had a
stroke. You should not be smoking.

Gordon Gordon Ahmffine.

Barry Gordon It's not going to aid your recovery is it?

Gordon Gordon Ischristmas.

Barry Gordon Honestly – you're mad, Mum'll do her
nut. It's not like the old days. Things have changed
around here since you left. You can't go blazing it up in
the front room on Christmas Day.

Gordon Gordon Is ma house.

Barry Gordon It's not your house any more. It's Mum's
house and, believe me, she takes a strong line on
recreational drug use.
    She's like Sweden in that respect.

*Barry sits down and inspects the joint. Eventually he
pops it behind his ear. He opens the* Sunday Times
Culture Section and begins flicking through it.

There's fuck-all on telly.
    Remember when Christmas TV used to be good?
    Dr Who's on.
    But the Christmas specials are always shit though,
aren't they?
    Remember that one with Kylie and that guy from
Stewarton in it? That was god-awful.

He's in *Coronation Street* now.

And this is David Tennant's last episode so it'll be a big syrupy, moist-eyed fiasco.

We should get Sky.

Gordon looks pained.

Ha! That's your Rupert Murdoch face. That's the same face you pulled when you found out Mum gets the *Sunday Times* now.

He waves the Culture Section provocatively at him.

Get over it, hippy, the revolution's over. You lost. In ten years the Rolling Stones will all be dead, the last two Beatles will be gone and it'll be like you lot never happened.

Maybe not McCartney though. He's immortal. Have you seen his lovely full head of believable, chestnutty hair? He looks younger and more vital than ever, doesn't he?

Barry gives a Macca thumbs-up.

What an idiot.

Aye, things change, old man. You may have weaselled your way back into the house but you're still sleeping downstairs and we're still getting the *Sunday Times*.

Have you got the remote control?

Gordon shakes his head.

Gordon Gordon G-g-g-give me my joint back.

Barry Gordon Shoosh, someone's coming.

Barry quickly stashes the joint out of sight. Norma enters. She is eighteen.

Oh, it's just you.

Norma Gordon Will you watch the wee man for me, Barry?

5

Barry Gordon Why can't Trevor do it?

Norma Gordon He's still not back from London.

Barry Gordon Still? I thought I heard him get in in the middle of the night.

Norma Gordon No.

Barry Gordon But it's Christmas Day.

Norma Gordon Oh really? Is that why there's a reindeer in the garden and Noel Edmunds is upstairs fingering Mum?

Barry Gordon Alright, Norma . . . steady on.

Norma Gordon Sorry, I just want to have a shower. I'm gross.

Barry Gordon Can you not just stick him on Dad's lap and leave him there with his boo-boo or something?

Norma Gordon No. Please, Barry?

Barry Gordon Where's Mum?

Norma Gordon Please going to just not be a dick, Barry?

Barry Gordon Alright, Norma. Seeing as it's Christmas. Have you seen the remote control?

Norma Gordon Thank you. No. He's in our room playing with his figures. Thank you. I smell disgusting.

She sniffs her top.

Honest to God. I smell like Glasgow.

Norma exits. Once she is out of the sitting room the light goes on in the small bathroom beside it. Norma enters. She is looking for something. She doesn't find it, so switches off the light and leaves.
Simultaneously, Barry gets up and has a look around for the remote control.

Barry Gordon Where's the remote control? This is weird. It's going to be really annoying if it doesn't turn up.

He exits. Gordon produces the remote control from down the side of his chair and puts on the TV.

Television . . . It's Christmas Day on STV and we've got a packed line-up of shows for your festive entertainment. First up we join Michelle McManus for . . .

Gordon switches it back off immediately. Irene Gordon enters.

Irene Gordon Right . . . The soup's made . . . The trifle's made . . . I've prepared all the vegetables except the Brussels . . . What's wrong with your face?

Gordon Gordon I'vehadastroke.

Irene Gordon Oh very droll, very droll. At least you've not lost that famous Cowardesque wit.
  Now, are we going to change your jumper before Robert gets here?

Gordon Gordon No.

Irene Gordon Yes, I think we should, it's Christmas Day and we're having company over. What about your nice blue one?

He doesn't answer.

Where's Norma?

Gordon Gordon Shower.

Irene Gordon Where's the wee man?

Gordon Gordon B-B-B-Barry's wathing him.

Irene Gordon Why on God's earth is Barry washing him?

Gordon Gordon WATHING. He'th *wathing* him.

Irene Gordon Oh, *watching* him. Right. Well that's bad enough. I'd better go and see if he's alright. No word from Trevor?

Gordon half shrugs.

It's Christmas Day, he's not going to get here now, is he? That's not a good sign, is it?

Gordon isn't interested.

Right, well, good talking to you, Gordon, I'll be in the other room making sure our son doesn't let our grandson eat pencils.

Norma enters.

Norma Gordon Mum – do you know where the good shampoo is?

Irene Gordon It's in the cupboard under the sink downstairs. If I don't hide it, Trevor uses it and it's not that I grudge him it, it's just he does use an awful lot of it.

Norma Gordon He's got big hair.

Irene Gordon He does.

Norma Gordon It's a ginge-fro.

Irene Gordon Have you left your son with his Uncle Barry?

Norma Gordon He'll be fine. I'm just having a shower.

Irene Gordon Barry's useless with him.

Norma Gordon Barry's useless.

Irene Gordon I'll go and stick my head in.

Norma Gordon Mum, he's fine.

Irene Gordon I'll just stick my head in.

Norma Gordon Mum!

Irene Gordon Norma – you know how you got that dent in your head.

Norma Gordon What dent in my head?

Irene puts her hand on the back of Norma's head and shows her.

That's not a dent.

Irene Gordon What would you call it?

Norma Gordon A contour.

Irene Gordon Well, you know how you got that contour.

Norma Gordon No.

Irene Gordon Oh well . . .

Norma Gordon How?

Irene Gordon Never mind.
I think there might be something wrong with wee Trevor.

Norma Gordon What did Barry do to my head?

Irene Gordon Nothing.

Norma Gordon Mum – what did he do?

Irene Gordon Nothing. It's fine.

Norma Gordon Well, it's not fine. Obviously it's not fine – there's a big weird dent in my head.

Irene Gordon I thought you said it was a contour?

Norma Gordon That was before I knew that Barry did it.

Irene Gordon You were just wee.

Norma Gordon What did he do?

Irene Gordon Nothing.

Norma Gordon MUM!

Irene Gordon I think there's something wrong with wee Trevor.

Gordon switches the TV back on.

Norma Gordon Oh. Right.

Irene Gordon You don't seem very concerned.

Norma Gordon I'm more worried about what Barry did to dent my head.

Irene Gordon Have you noticed anything?

Norma Gordon I noticed there was a contour.

Irene Gordon About Trevor!

Norma Gordon I don't spend all my spare time scrutinising him like you do. I feed him and leave him to it.

Irene Gordon He's coughing.

Norma Gordon No, he isn't.

Irene Gordon He is. He's got a fever. Are you listening?

Norma is fascinated by something on the TV.

Norma Gordon Is that Matt Lucas?

Gordon Gordon Mithelle McManuth.

Norma Gordon Oh aye, so it is. It's an easy mistake to make though, isn't it but?

Irene Gordon NORMA!

Norma Gordon Uh-huh?

Irene Gordon Aren't you even a little bit concerned about wee Trevor?

Norma Gordon Honestly, Mum, you worry about him too much. I'm sure he's fine.

Irene Gordon What if he dies when big Trevor's away?

Norma Gordon He won't die. You're paranoid. I'm going for a shower. Stop biffing out.

Irene Gordon I think his feathers are falling out.

Norma Gordon What am I meant to do?

Irene Gordon He's your Trevor's chicken.

Norma Gordon He's a cock.

Irene Gordon He's sensitive.

Norma Gordon I mean wee Trevor's a cock.

Irene Gordon So do I. Wee Trevor's sensitive. Anyway – cock, chicken, rooster, hen, chooky . . . whatever he is. What if he dies before your Trevor gets back from London?

Norma Gordon I don't think he'll suspect us of poultricide, Mum.

Irene Gordon He might. It's Christmas. And if he's not here to see what we have for dinner. He's very fond of that bird.

Norma Gordon I know he is. They're soul mates – one man and his cock. It's like that film with Clint Eastwood and the monkey.

Gordon Gordon Ith not a monkey . . .

Norma Gordon Wee Trevor's Clint Eastwood though, but obviously . . . Big Trevor's the monkey.

Gordon Gordon Ithnae a monkey. Ith an orangutan.

Norma Gordon Wee Trevor is not going to die. He's fine. He's not off his food, is he? And he was up bright and early annoying the whole street this morning as usual. Waking up the wee man so I had to get up. I resent having my life dictated to by a chicken who doesn't even lay eggs.

Irene Gordon Och, that's not Trevor's fault.

Norma Gordon Not wee Trevor's fault, no, it's big Trevor's fault. Who buys a cockerel for the garden?

Irene Gordon He didn't know it was, did he? They all look the same when they're babies. Like wee wisps of yellow candy floss.

Norma Gordon Aye, right – buying a cockerel's a mistake but keeping a cockerel once you've realised is just mental. We should have Kentucky-fried it then and there and been done with it.

Irene Gordon They were pals by then.

Norma Gordon IT'S A CHICKEN!

Irene Gordon Any news on Trevor?

Norma Gordon I thought you said he had a cough and was moulting.

Irene Gordon Big Trevor.

Norma Gordon No.

Irene Gordon And his mobile's still switched off?

Norma Gordon *Uh-huh!*

Irene Gordon I'm just asking.

Norma Gordon And I'm just saying. Do you want a copy of his itinerary? He had an interview on the 23rd and he missed his flight back because he got on the wrong tube line twice, and all the buses and trains and planes are booked. So he's stuck till tomorrow.

Irene Gordon But has he got somewhere to stay?

Norma Gordon *Yes!* He's sleeping on someone's couch.

Irene Gordon Who's letting him sleep on their couch at Christmas?

Norma Gordon I don't know. Some guy.
   He'll be here tomorrow, ask him then.

Irene Gordon Poor Trevor.

Norma Gordon Poor Norma. I'm the one left with grotbags to look after on my own while he gads about London.

Irene Gordon Hardly on your own. And I've never seen your Trevor gadding about anywhere. Do you know how he got on at the interview?

Norma Gordon No.

Irene Gordon I hope he doesn't get it. And I know that's awfully selfish of me, but it's true. I don't want you all moving down to London. I know he hates it at the roll factory but he'll get something in Kilmarnock. Or Irvine. Or Glasgow.

Norma Gordon They don't publish comics in Kilmarnock or Irvine or Glasgow.

Irene Gordon Well I'm sure there's a middle ground between bridies and *Batman*.

Norma Gordon It isn't *Batman*.

Irene Gordon I know, Norma – I'm not completely disconnected. Now do you think your dad should change his jumper before Robert gets here?

13

Norma Gordon It's Rab, Mum, not Robert.

Irene Gordon Well, do you think I should change your father's jumper before Rab gets here then?

Norma Gordon I don't know. You can put him in a tutu for all Rab'll care.

Right – anyway . . . I'm going for a shower.

Norma exits.

Irene Gordon There's definitely something she's not telling me. Gordon, are you listening?

Gordon Gordon Uh-huh.

Irene Gordon And it's a shame he isnae here. Because this is going to be nice today, isn't it? You pretend it's just a piece of nonsense, don't you? Christmas. That it's just an excuse for presents and everything, but it's years like this that you really appreciate it. And I know we've got them here all the time, but still – it's nice to have your family around you, isn't it? At Christmas.

Gordon Gordon Yeth. Ahma velly luchy man.

Irene Gordon You are. We're all lucky. The wee man's really going to enjoy this Christmas, isn't he? He was a bit wee last year – not that you'll remember.

Gordon Gordon Irene . . .

Irene Gordon I'm not having a dig. I'm just saying. You weren't here. He was. He was just a wee red-headed blob staring at everything. He'll enjoy it this year.

Right, I'd better go and rescue him from Barry.

Gordon Gordon Yousmotherhim.

Irene Gordon I mother him? I'm his granny.

Gordon Gordon S-s-s-s-s-smother.

Irene Gordon I'm his granny, I'm supposed to.

Gordon Gordon Barry. Y-y-y-y-you smother Barry.

Irene Gordon If he doesn't want smothered he can move out. And wouldn't that be a prayer answered?

She exits. Gordon watches her leave and immediately starts trying to put a joint together again. This time, though, he uses both hands. He is suddenly interrupted by Irene returning, marching Barry back into the lounge. Gordon quickly hides his paraphernalia back in his little box.

Are you mentally defective?

She indicates that he sit down.

Barry Gordon I'm a grown man.

Irene Gordon Ha! And even if you were – Wee Gordon's a baby.

Barry Gordon He's a toddler.

Irene Gordon Don't. Just don't, Barry. Gordon – you will not believe what he was doing –

Barry Gordon I think he might.

Irene Gordon . . . in front of our grandson. Do you want to give him brain damage too?

Barry Gordon I don't have brain damage.

Irene Gordon Your father does.

Gordon Gordon I d-d-d-d-d-don't have –

Irene Gordon And do you think all that wacky baccy he smoked all those years had nothing to do with his condition? Think on, Barry.

Gordon Gordon I d-d-d-d-d-don't have brain damage.

Irene Gordon He was smoking a joint of marijuana. In the same room Wee Gordon was playing with his figures.

Barry Gordon Out the window. I was smoking it out the window.

Irene Gordon This is too much, Barry. You've crossed a line.

Barry Gordon I was smoking it out the window.

Irene Gordon I don't care if you were smoking it out your bahooki . . . You were in charge of Wee Gordon.

Barry Gordon It's not a big deal.

Irene Gordon Not a big deal? Have you pickled your brain so badly that you can't see what's wrong with this? You were in charge of Wee Gordon. He's a baby. He needs a responsible adult watching him at all times . . .

It dawns on her that she has left Wee Gordon unattended.

Gordon, you better talk some sense into your son because I am losing control here!
    Gordon! Are you listening to me?

Gordon Gordon Uh-huh.

Irene Gordon Right. Deal with him.

She exits.

Gordon Gordon Y-y-y-y-y –

Barry Gordon Don't. Just don't. I don't want to hear it.

Gordon Gordon – you're a stupid bastard.

Barry Gordon The apple doesn't fall far from the tree, does it?

Gordon Gordon You need to sober up.

Barry Gordon Why? I've got nothing to sober up for. It's the economy – we're a lost generation. You baby-boomers have drunk the well dry.

Gordon Gordon You shouldnae h-h-h-huv d-d-d-dropped out.

Barry Gordon I hated it. It was shit. What's the point anyway? Even if I stayed to get my degree I'd be worse off at the end of it. Six grand worse off. More.

Gordon Gordon You need to get a job.

Barry Gordon There are no jobs. What, work in the roll factory with Trevor? No thanks.

Gordon Gordon Y-y-y-your mother –

Barry Gordon I know it's Christmas and everything, but honestly, if you think I'm going to listen to a lecture from you about smoking weed then I think the stroke must have been more serious than we thought.

Gordon Gordon Just don't do it in front of the baby.

Barry Gordon I get it. I know.

Gordon Gordon Your mother is –

Barry Gordon *I know*. Alright? Look, I know. I shouldn't have done it. It was stupid. I get it, but if you think it's appropriate for you to start coming the concerned father then you need to get real.

Gordon Gordon Bally . . .

Barry Gordon Even before you ran off and left Mum you were a crap dad.

Gordon Gordon I know. I know that.

Barry Gordon And I'm not buying this reformed sinner act either. I think the only one who does believe it is

Norma, but she's always had a blind spot when it comes to you.

Gordon Gordon It's a squint, son, isnae a blind spot.

The doorbell goes.

Barry Gordon Who's that?

Gordon Gordon R-R-R-R-Rab McGuire . . .

Barry Gordon What?

Irene shouts through from the other room:

Irene Gordon CAN SOMEONE ANSWER THE DOOR?

Gordon Gordon On you go.

Barry Gordon You are joking?
It's Christmas Day.

Gordon Gordon Y-y-y-y-y-you really n-n-n-n-need to get over tha lathie.

Barry Gordon I'm over her. I don't care. She's a bitch anyway. What kind of pal steals your bird?

Gordon Gordon If you leave her lying around.

Barry Gordon I was on holiday.

Gordon Gordon For a year.

Barry Gordon I'm not interested in relationship advice from you.

Gordon Gordon You're not interested in any advice from anyone.

Barry Gordon Although you are unusually well qualified to offer advice on dating teenage girls, for a man of your age.

The doorbell goes again. Irene shouts again –

Irene Gordon DON'T PUSH ME, BARRY. GET. THE. DOOR.

Barry gets up and exits to answer the door, muttering.

Barry Gordon Fucksakeman.

Gordon opens his little box, realises it's an impossible dream with the house this busy and puts it away.
Barry enters, Rab follows him. Barry immediately sits down and glares at the TV, ignoring Rab.

Rab McGuire Hello there, Mr Gordon.

Gordon Gordon H-h-h-h-hello.

Rab McGuire You feeling alright aye?

Gordon Gordon Bllilliant.

Rab McGuire Great. Barry?

Barry ignores him.

What's poppin?

He ignores him.

Gordon Gordon He's got his pelliod.

Rab McGuire Michelle said to me the other day she'd missed her period – I said, 'We aw feel like that, pet, but what's the chances of being born in the jazz age or during punk or the renaissance or . . .'

He tails off, embarrassed.

Right, aye, maybe no appropriate.

Gordon Gordon Sit down.

He does.

Rab McGuire She hasnae missed her period either, but . . . By the way. Em, just so you . . . Em . . . it was just a wee joke . . . sorry.

Silence.

What did the epileptic get for Christmas?

They don't answer.

A wee fit!

Silence.

This is very good of you to have me over, Mr G. I said to Mrs G that I was happy in myself with a Chinese but she was awfy insistent. Your wife's a difficult woman to say no to . . .

Gordon Gordon Aye.

Barry Gordon You find it difficult to say no to all the women though, ay, Rab?

Rab McGuire Barry, man – it's Christmas.

Barry Gordon I know it is. It's my house. It's my Christmas. And yet – there you are.

Rab McGuire Aye, here I am. Listen, man, I'm sorry, I've said I'm sorry.

Barry Gordon I don't know why I'm surprised, though – my house, my girlfriend, my Christmas . . . you batter in, make yourself at home, help yourself.

Rab McGuire Barry man, that was two years ago.

Gordon Gordon He's still upset. He's s-s-s-s-s-sensitive. Like a n-n-n-n-n-nipple.

Rab McGuire Barry – do we have to talk about this in front of your dad?

Barry Gordon We don't have to talk about it at all.

Rab McGuire We were pals and I messed that up – I get it.

Barry Gordon Now you get it?

Rab McGuire But Barry – with the wee man and everything – now we're family you're going to have to get over it. It was years ago, man.

Barry Gordon Sure. You're right. It's forgotten.

Rab McGuire Really?

Barry Gordon No, not really. You stole her off me.

Rab McGuire Point one: as a feminist I refute categorically the notion that a woman can be stolen. Point two: as Stewarton's original brilliant-orange G-pimp, hustler, mac – extraordinaire . . .
   Barry man, hate the game, not the player.

Barry Gordon You're a tool.

Rab McGuire Och, come on, man, what's done is done. Really, really, I am truly sorry. Bro's before ho's. I get it. But can you no gie me a wee pass for past-nastification and can we no just start over? New beginnings and aw that?

Barry Gordon No.

Rab McGuire I think that's very sad. You two were weans when you went out. You'd be bored of her by now anyway. Trust me.

Norma enters. She is done up to the nines. Rab immediately stands up to welcome her.

There she is – wee Norma – the sexiest sister-in-law in Stewarton. East Ayrshire's sweetheart.

Norma Gordon Oh Rab.

They hug.

Have the boys been looking after you?

Rab McGuire Oh aye – we've been having a piss laugh. So . . . where's my favourite nephew hanging?

Norma Gordon Barry's looking after him.

She looks at Barry.

Barry Gordon Mum's with him.

Norma Gordon Do you want to come up and see him?

Rab McGuire Aye, man – course I do. Is he not coming down no?

Norma Gordon I want him to have a wee nap before lunch. Wee Trevor woke him up at God-knows-what o'clock with all his crowing.

Rab McGuire Haw-haw. Wee Trevor man. Whit a dick.

Norma Gordon He is a cock.

Rab McGuire Exactly, man. Whit a cock. You heard from Big Trevor yet today?

Norma Gordon Not yet.

Rab McGuire Do you know how he got on at his interview? Aside fae missing the bus, obviously. Only Trevor, man . . .

Norma Gordon I think he thought it went quite well, but he doesn't know.

Rab McGuire Och, He'll skoosh it. If he can get a job in a roll factory with those fingernails he can get a job drawing. Brother's a braw drawer.

Norma Gordon Well, we'll see.

Barry Gordon Fingers crossed. If you all move to London I can get my bedroom back.

Norma Gordon Barry – you're twenty-two – you don't think you should move out?

Barry Gordon I thought the whole point in being a teen mum was getting your own council house.

Norma Gordon Ah'm no living up the junky flats beside the school. Why don't you get a junky flat beside the school?

Barry Gordon I don't have a job.

Norma Gordon Why don't you get a job?

Barry Gordon The economy.

Norma Gordon That's your answer to everything – isnae the economy that gets you stoned every day. Come on, Rab.

Rab and Norma exit to see Wee Gordon.

Barry Gordon I can't believe he's here. This is the worst Christmas ever.

Gordon Gordon D-d-d-d-d-dry your i-i-i-i-i-eyes.

Barry Gordon How come the telly's on? Have you got the remote control?

Lights up on Norma and Rab cramming themselves into the tiny downstairs toilet. Rab sits on the lavatory and Norma stands over him. They kiss like they're trying to eat each other. Norma breaks away.

Norma Gordon No. We can't do this any more.

Rab McGuire I know, we shouldnae start if we cannae finish.

He thinks.

We cannae get finished now, no?

Norma Gordon NO!

Rab McGuire Aye, you're right, we'd better go and see the wee man.

Norma Gordon No. I mean any more. At all.

Rab McGuire What?

Norma Gordon I've been thinking. I'm serious. I'm sorry, Rab. I need to give Trevor and me another chance.

Rab McGuire How many chances are you going to gie it? You two are like a game of Monopoly you've given it that many chances. Is it no about time for a community chest?

He grabs her chest.

Norma Gordon Don't. I'm sorry, Rab. You know how I feel.

Rab McGuire Exactly.

Norma Gordon But he's Wee Gordon's dad.

Rab McGuire Where is he?

Norma Gordon He got stuck in London.

Rab McGuire Aye.

Norma Gordon He did.

Rab McGuire Aye.

Norma Gordon *He did!* You know he got on the wrong tube.

Rab McGuire Twice.

Norma Gordon Look, anyway, my mind's made up.

Rab McGuire Fine.

Norma Gordon Please, let me explain, Rab, it isn't that I don't love you, you know I –

Rab McGuire Let's just not talk about it then. You've made a decision. It's Christmas. Let's not talk about it – for the wean and your family.

They gaze at each other in silent anguish.

You're making a colossal mistake.

Norma Gordon I thought we just weren't talking about it.

Rab McGuire He's my brother.

Norma Gordon Exactly.

Rab McGuire Exactly. It's my family that's going to be fucked apart – not yours, they don't even like Trevor.

Norma Gordon My mum does.

Rab McGuire Maws like everyone. They couldnae care less.

Norma Gordon Except Barry.

Rab McGuire Fuck Barry.

Norma Gordon He heard you come round last night – he thought it was Trevor. This is too much. It's all too much.

Rab McGuire Barry's got fuck-all to do with it from where I'm standing.

Norma Gordon Sitting.

Rab McGuire Sitting. I fucking love you, Norma.

Norma Gordon Don't.

Rab McGuire Listen . . .

Norma Gordon Don't.

Rab McGuire Please. I love you like a force of nature. Like a tsunami. I love you like a tsunami.

Norma Gordon You loved Michelle.

Rab McGuire I never did.

Norma Gordon You live with her!

Rab McGuire So? That was a mistake. Now we're just like any other flatmates – pure simmering resentment, fighting over the dishes and the remote control. I'll leave her today, now, this second. I don't care. I just want you, Norma. I just want you.

Norma Gordon You loved Vera Iqbal.

Rab McGuire Come on tae fuck! I was fifteen! It's only you. What do I have to do to prove it? Do you want me to get a tattoo on my face? I fucking will. I'll get a big tattoo that says 'I fucking love Norma Gordon' right across my big stupid face.

Norma Gordon Just stop now.

Rab McGuire I can't stop.

Norma Gordon You'll have to. You'll have to right now before anyone hears and you'll just have to, have to because it's never going to happen. You're Wee Gordon's uncle.

Rab McGuire *So?*

Norma Gordon So? Imagine what they'd say at the Co-op! I don't want to be some Jenny Kyle.

Rab McGuire Don't be such a tit.

Norma Gordon Did you just call me a tit?

Rab McGuire What we have is special, Norma – it fucking transcends that shit.

Norma Gordon It's easy for you to say – you live in Glasgow. I live in Stewarton.

Rab McGuire It isnae about Stewarton, Norma. This is our destiny – you and me.

Norma Gordon Don't.

Rab McGuire When we're together I could almost believe in a cognitive God.

Norma Gordon Rab . . .

Rab McGuire But it isn't God. It's stronger than God, it's our Darwinian imperative . . . natural selection.

Norma Gordon Rab . . .

Rab McGuire We've selected each other and you know what I'm talking about. It's evolution. When we come it's like fucking fish evolving into monkeys evolving into homo sapiens. All in one second.

Norma Gordon I've told you – that happens to everyone sometimes . . .

Rab McGuire Very funny. Laugh it up.

Knock at the door.

Irene Gordon Hello – Norma? Are you in there, Norma?

Norma Gordon Em. Yes. Hold on a minute.

Irene Gordon Gordon needs changing, he's had an accident.

Norma Gordon What one?

Irene Gordon The wee one.

Norma Gordon Hold on, I'll be out in a second.

Rab kisses her. She responds.

You're a homo sapien.

Rab McGuire We can leave Stewarton.

Irene enters the lounge.

Irene Gordon Was that Robert at the door?

Barry Gordon Why didn't you tell me he was coming?

Irene Gordon I wasn't aware you needed to approve the guest list.

Barry Gordon Mum – you know I hate him.

Irene Gordon Stop being a child, Barry.

Barry Gordon It's Christmas . . .

Irene Gordon Listen to yourself – oh, you're your father's son alright. Me me me. I didn't tell you because of all . . . this. Because of how I knew you'd react. It's none of your business. It's my house. I'll invite who I like.

Barry Gordon He's a dick.

Irene Gordon You and Norma are only here because of my indulgence. Other people's kids move out, you know. You do know other people's kids move out? And when most women's husbands leave they don't come back. My nest just keeps getting fuller.
  Robert's Wee Gordon's uncle.

Barry Gordon Exactly – he's only his uncle. I can't remember the last time I saw any of my weird uncles. Why can't he just send tokens?

Irene Gordon He dotes on him.

Barry Gordon Can't I at least just have Christmas Day without him? Why can't he have Christmas with his own family?

Irene Gordon We are his family. Anyway – we didn't know Trevor would be held up, did we?

Barry Gordon His *real* family?

Irene Gordon The McGuires are away skiing and his Michelle is away on Mull with her mum and her new man.

Barry Gordon She's a lesbian.

Irene Gordon Not any more.

Gordon Gordon Sheeth b-b-b-back on tholids.

Irene Gordon She's reformed.

Barry Gordon I knew that evangelical church in Barassie would cause trouble.

Irene Gordon She's been seeing this guy for about a year now. He's a surgeon.

Gordon Gordon H-h-h-h-he's a tree surgeon.

Barry Gordon Old Alice must be spinning in her cardboard coffin.

Irene Gordon Seriously, Barry – don't push me today. I am this close.

She shows him how close.

This close. Did you talk to him?

Gordon Gordon Uh-huh.

Irene Gordon Well, this isn't over. You and I are going to have a serious conversation after Robert leaves. That was unacceptable, Barry. Un. Axe. Eptable.

Barry Gordon Right.

Irene Gordon I don't want you to smoke that stuff in this house ever again. Anywhere. Do you understand?

Barry Gordon Uh-huh.

Irene Gordon Anywhere. In this house. Ever again. And you're out. Do you understand?

Barry Gordon YES.

Irene Gordon You're twenty-two now, for God's sake. You need to grow up. Where is Robert?

Barry Gordon Looking at Wee Gordon with Norma.

Norma enters.

Norma Gordon I can't believe he's still doing that.

Irene Gordon He's just wee.

Norma Gordon He's nearly one and a half. The books said he'd be potty-trained by now. I don't even think he bothers.

Barry Gordon A bad teacher blames her students.

Norma Gordon Shut up, Barry.

Irene Gordon Where's Robert?

Norma Gordon He's watching Wee Gordon.

Irene Gordon Och, he's awful good with him.

Barry Gordon Alright, Mum, you've made your point.

Norma Gordon I don't think the wee man's feeling that well. I'm going to try and put him down for a couple of hours.

Irene Gordon Oh, the wee lamb. Give him a kiss from Granny. Right. Now Robert's here I'm going to get the potatoes on.

Irene exits.

Barry Gordon Why is he here?

Norma Gordon His mum and dad are away skiing.

Barry Gordon So? Why's he our problem?

Norma Gordon He's Wee Gordon's uncle.

Barry Gordon Fff.

Norma Gordon Seriously, Barry – get over it. Are you still gurning about Michelle Montgomery? God. That was two years ago.

Barry Gordon We were pals and he stole my bird.

Norma Gordon Stole your bird – get real, Barry, what age are you?

Barry Gordon It's indicative of his moral character.

Norma Gordon And what does sitting around in your pyjamas all day smoking weed and wanking indicate about yours?

Barry Gordon That's not all I do.

Norma Gordon No, you play Football Manager too. You're a real power house. You better check yourself before you wreck yourself, Barry.

Barry Gordon Will everyone just get off my case? It's Christmas! I'm thinking through my options.

Norma Gordon Wank or smoke, smoke or wank, wank or smoke . . .
Sorry, Dad.

Gordon Gordon Fine.

Rab enters.

Rab McGuire Awright, Gordons. That wee guy is amazing. What a wee player. He just called me Unco. Unco – man, can you believe it?

Norma Gordon He loves his Unco Rab.

Rab McGuire And his Unco Rab loves him. Whit a wee brammer he is. He's got a nice wide McGuire face.

Barry Gordon His head's like a deflated pumpkin.

Norma Gordon No it isn't. He's fine. Normal. Nice. He's nice looking.

Barry Gordon Whatever. So have you got the remote?

Gordon doesn't answer.

Right. Fuck this. Maybe it's in the kitchen.

He exits to look for it.

Norma Gordon Who's watching grotbags?

Rab McGuire Em, I just left him on his own.

Norma Gordon Rab!

Rab McGuire Sorry, he seemed fine. He's in his wee baby prison thing.

Norma gets up.

Norma Gordon Given he cannae even control his bowels he's pretty good at breaking out his baby prison. Like the Bird Baby of Alcatraz.

Rab McGuire I'll come with you.

Norma Gordon *Don't . . .*
You keep Dad company.

She exits. They sit together in awkward silence for a moment.

Rab McGuire So . . . do you have the remote control? There must be something better than . . . Is that Matt Lucas?

Gordon Gordon It's Michelle McManus.

Rab McGuire Oh, right enough.

Silence.

Gordon Gordon Can you roll joints, Rab?

Rab McGuire Joints? Em . . . how do you mean?

Gordon Gordon Spliffs, doobies, jays.

Rab McGuire Joints. Right. Em . . . can I roll joints? I'm the big roller. How?

Gordon Gordon What does that mean?

Rab McGuire Em. Aye. I can. Aye.

He hands him the box.

Gordon Gordon Go and roll me a j-j-j-j-joint.

Rab McGuire Em . . . are you sure? I mean – is that a good idea? Christmas Day . . .

Gordon Gordon It's fine.

Rab McGuire Right, sorry, aye. Everything in here aye? All the, em . . . fixings?
Right. Aye. Em. Alright.

He exits. Gordon stands up and stretches. He does a couple of lunges and shakes the pins and needles out of his legs.
Rab enters the downstairs toilet and rolls a joint for Gordon.
Meanwhile the lounge door opens and Gordon dives back into his wheelchair. Barry enters.

Barry Gordon I still can't find it. Have you definitely not seen it?

Gordon grunts.

Well, what a shite Christmas this is. Rab's here and I can't find the remote control. I bet my presents are shit too.

Gordon turns up the volume and changes the channel.

I knew you had it. Give us it here.

Gordon Gordon Fugg off.

Barry Gordon *The Muppets Take Manhattan* is on.

Gordon Gordon Don't care.

Barry Gordon You are quite the prick, Dad.
    You're awfully lucky you had that stroke because there is no way Mum would have taken you back if you hadn't. No way.

Gordon Gordon D-d-d-don't push it, son.

Barry Gordon I was glad when you left. You've been a useless father, a useless husband and a useless man for as long as I remember.

Irene enters holding a blue sweater for Gordon to change into.

Irene Gordon Can you come and give me a hand with the Brussels, Barry?

Barry Gordon Sure.

He gets up.

Irene Gordon Wow. I expected the usual protracted negotiation.

Barry Gordon No. Happy to help you, Mum.

Irene Gordon Well, they're just sitting beside the sink. Do about seven each. Except for your father, because he doesn't like them.

Barry Gordon None of us like them.

Irene Gordon They're fun-sized cabbages – what's not to like?

Barry Gordon That. They're just, like, wee cabbages.

Irene Gordon Think of them as cabbage nanos if that helps. Anyway, the rest of you will eat what you're given.

Barry Gordon Fine.

Irene Gordon Do the wee crosses on the bottom, remember.

He exits.

How are you feeling?

Gordon Gordon Fwine.

Irene Gordon Och, he's a good boy really, isn't he?

Gordon Gordon Hmph.

Irene Gordon Kids are all like that – all groin and no brain. Look at our Norma. Barry's just a bit delicate. He'll be fine though, won't he?

Gordon Gordon Uh-huh.

Irene Gordon I wish he didn't smoke those . . .

Gordon Gordon Thorry.

Irene Gordon It's like he's given up on life.

Gordon Gordon Thorry.

Irene Gordon Oh Gordon, I don't blame you. I blame myself. I let you. I was an enabler. And look how you've ended up.

Gordon Gordon Isnaecosismoked.

Irene Gordon Och you say that, Gordon, but we'll never know. And I'll tell you what else didn't help? When you left and were spending all your time drinking and slipping on ecstasies in the Stewarton Arms. And I'm not just saying that because of you running around with that wee barmaid either. I'm not. Honestly, Gordon, I could not care less. Although – what were you thinking? There's no fool like an old fool.

Gordon looks at her.

Look at Paul McCartney.

Rab is finished rolling the joint. He switches out the light and leaves the bathroom.

Right. Let's get you changed.

Gordon Gordon Ahmfine.

Irene Gordon It's Christmas Day, Gordon. Just because . . . you're not well . . . it's still Christmas. Let's get you looking a bit jazzy.

Gordon Gordon Jazz'sshite.

Irene Gordon Jazz is shite, but looking jazzy isnae. Come on. Arm up.

Reluctantly Gordon raises his right arm and Irene helps him out his jumper. He is wearing just his vest when Rab enters. waving the joint he has rolled.

Rab McGuire Right, all sorted . . .

He spots Gordon's state of undress and Irene's presence and stashes the joint in his pocket.

Eh, I mean . . .

Irene Gordon Oh hello, Robert.

Rab McGuire Hiyya, Mrs Gordon. Will I give you two a wee bit of . . . em . . . privacy?

Irene Gordon Och no, you're fine, Robert, I'm just changing Gordon's sweater.

Rab McGuire I can just go and see what Norma's up to with the wee man.

Irene Gordon No, no, come on in, sit down.

Rab McGuire Okay . . .

Irene Gordon In fact, could you give me a wee hand?

Rab McGuire Em. Aye? No bother.

Irene Gordon Could you just hold up his left arm and I'll pop the jumper on. Don't worry, he doesn't mind – do you, Gordon?

Gordon Gordon Yeth.

Irene Gordon Anyway –

Rab McGuire Alright. Em, so I just hold it by the, eh, by the wrist?

Irene Gordon Thanks, Robert, just give it a right good howk up.

The put the jumper on.

There. Now that's better. That's the Tariq Ali of the Kilmarnock Academy woodwork department that I . . .

She catches herself.

Anyway . . .

Rab McGuire Were you a techy teacher, Mr G?

Gordon nods.

Haw-haw. Brilliant man. I can just see you in one of they wee broon white coats.

Irene Gordon Never trust a teacher who wears a costume, Robert. Techy, science, PE – they're the worst ones going.

Rab McGuire You're an English teacher, Mrs G?

Irene Gordon That's right.

Rab McGuire Where is it you teach? Maybole?

Irene Gordon Louden.

Rab McGuire English as a foreign language then, aye? Techy teachers are a weird lot but aren't they, no?

Gordon looks like he disagrees.

Not that you are . . . I mean . . . I didn't mean that . . .

Irene Gordon You're absolutely right, Robert, they are a weird, weird lot. I'll be in the kitchen. Would you boys like a drink?

Rab McGuire That would be magic, Mrs G, I can get them but.

Irene Gordon Not at all. You're a guest. Gordon?

He nods.

Right, coming up.

Rab McGuire So. Techy ay? I think I've still got a spice rack I made in techy. That's just what a fourteen-year-old boy wants in'tit? A spice rack.

Gordon switches the TV on. Norma enters.

Norma Gordon That's him crashed out. Finally. Have you two been getting on?

Rab McGuire Oh aye – like a burning building.

Norma Gordon How are you feeling, Dad?

Gordon Gordon Fine.

Norma Gordon That's good.

Barry enters with two small glasses of sherry for Rab and Gordon.

Barry Gordon Sherry.

Rab McGuire Right. Yes it is. Brilliant. Sherry.

He hands it to Rab.

Thanks.

He hands the other to Gordon.

Sherry . . .

Barry Gordon Do you want a drink, Norma?

Norma Gordon Not sherry I don't. Sherry is howking.

Barry Gordon What do you want?

Norma Gordon Have we got any Shloer?

Barry Gordon Dad's got a Shloer.

Norma Gordon That's not funny, Barry. He's disabled.

Barry Gordon I think there's some Appletise.

Norma Gordon That's fine. I'll have an Appletise.

Barry exits.

Rab McGuire Well. Here we are.

Norma Gordon Yeah. Here we are.

Rab McGuire Christmas ay?

Norma Gordon Yeh. Christmas.

All three of them sit and gaze at the TV in silence.
Barry returns with a drink for Norma and a beer for
himself.

Barry Gordon *The Muppets* are on.

Rab McGuire Haw-haw, excellent. What one?

Barry Gordon *Take Manhattan.*

Rab McGuire Amazing.

Barry Gordon I know. It's the Muppets' *Empire Strikes*
Back.

Rab McGuire Em . . . no, it isnae.

Barry Gordon Sorry?

Rab McGuire Em, it isnae the Muppets' *Empire Strikes Back*, it's the Muppets' *Return of the Jedi*.

Barry Gordon Oh, really?

Rab McGuire Em, aye, sorry. *The Great Muppet Caper* is the muppets' *Empire Strikes Back*. It's the second one.

Barry Gordon But it's the best one.

Rab McGuire Eh, alright, naw . . .

Gordon Gordon You two are muppets.

Irene enters.

Irene Gordon Right. That's everything, I think. We'll eat after the Queen's speech . . .

Gordon pulls a face – she points at him.

Don't you say a word, Gordon Gordon. I spent twenty-odd years not watching the Queen's speech and the monarchy hasn't been overthrown in a bloody coup – so I don't feel like my checking in with Liz and the weans on Christmas Day is going to make much of a difference.

Barry Gordon I'm starving.

Irene Gordon Well, go and have an apple.

Barry Gordon I don't want an apple.

Irene Gordon Well, I'm sorry we don't keep more of your favourite things on hand for you. Maybe you could get a job, buy your own food, and then you can eat what you like when you like, but as it is you'll eat what I give you when I give you it.

Barry Gordon You're just trying to show off in front of Rab.

Irene Gordon Show off?

Barry Gordon Pretend you're all middle class.

Irene Gordon I'm sorry?

Barry Gordon The later you eat the more middle class you are.

Norma Gordon That's true.

Barry Gordon And we've always been tea with *Neighbours*.

Irene Gordon What time do your family eat, Robert?

Rab McGuire Em . . .

Barry Gordon I bet they eat at nine o'clock and I bet they call it supper.

Rab McGuire No, em, we usually eat about seven.

Irene Gordon I wouldn't like that. I get home from school at four o'clock and I'm starving. I struggle to wait until five sometimes.

Barry Gordon You call your tea 'supper', though, don't you?

Rab McGuire No. We call it dinner. Anyway – I don't live there any more and I have my tea at six and I call it my tea.

Barry Gordon Tell us more about your reverse social mobility.

Irene Gordon Barry.

Barry Gordon You phoney.

Irene Gordon Barry, please.

Barry Gordon You're so plastic you're see-through.

Irene Gordon Barry, I'm serious. Stop it now or you can just leave.

Barry Gordon Fine.

Irene Gordon I'm sorry, Robert.
   Apologise.

Barry Gordon Sorry.

Rab McGuire No worries. Lively discourse. This is what it's all about. Em. Mrs Gordon, I can just head up the road you know. I honestly don't mind grabbing a sweet and sour king prawn from the Oriental Palace.

Norma Gordon Ooo get him, Barry. Has to have a king prawn . . . he's a prawn-monarchist.

Irene Gordon Don't be silly, Rab.

Rab McGuire I don't want to ruin your Christmas.

Irene Gordon Ruin Christmas? It'll be a relief to get a decent conversation for once. Between Cheech and Chong and Lady Gaga there I end up spending most of my time talking to your brother's chicken.

Rab McGuire How is wee Trevor?

Norma Gordon Don't start her.

Irene Gordon I don't think he's well, Rab. Do you know anything about chickens?

Rab McGuire Nothing – I couldn't even show you where the nuggets are.

Irene Gordon Have you heard from Big Trevor yet today?

Rab McGuire He called my folks but I don't think they talked to him for long cos they were having a fondue.

Norma Gordon Don't, Barry.

Irene Gordon Are they having a nice time?

Rab McGuire Magic.

Irene Gordon Poor Trevor. Your heart goes out to him, doesn't it? All on his own at Christmas.

Rab McGuire Ach he'll be fine. He's at his pals'.

Barry Gordon What pals does he have in London?

Rab McGuire Gonk's working in London now.

Norma Gordon What's he doing?

Rab McGuire He's a bogus gas man. It's no the greatest career but on balance it's better than being a real gas man.

Barry Gordon Since when was Trevor a pal of Gonk's?

Rab McGuire Facebook, man, no one is lonely any more. Everyone's at it. I'm pals wi Dixon McCurdie, Sponge Bob Shit Pants and Mr Iqbal – it's a total melting pot.

Barry Gordon But Gonk?

Rab McGuire Oh aye. And he's pure digi-Gonk these days, aye twittering. He's got a blog.

Norma Gordon I didnae know Gonk's got a blog.

Rab McGuire Www.gonkthoughts.blogspot.com.

Barry Gordon That'll be a short read.

Rab McGuire No, he's a changed man now. Ever since he came out he's transformed – like he's burst oot a plooky chrysalis. He's all erudite and witty.

Barry Gordon Came out of what? No way was Gonk in the army.

Rab McGuire Naw man, he's gay.

Barry Gordon Gonk's gay? No way.

Norma Gordon As gay as a goose.

Rab McGuire As queer as a duck.

Barry Gordon But he's only got one ball.

Norma Gordon So? Handicaps can be gay too.

Rab McGuire He's a monosticular homosexual.

Barry Gordon Wow.

Norma Gordon How did you not know that, Barry?

Barry Gordon I don't know.

Norma Gordon Do you never talk to anyone?

Barry Gordon Like who?

Norma Gordon Like anyone?

Barry Gordon I talk to people.

Norma Gordon Who? 'Pals fae travelling' hip-pies! Total hip-pies. Do you never talk to anyone fae Stewarton?

Barry Gordon Not really.

Norma Gordon Saaad.

Barry Gordon I sometimes see Ricky Mitchell.

Norma Gordon I bet you do. Slick Rick?

She makes a smoking gesture and a deep inhale.

Barry Gordon Shut up, Norma.

Irene Gordon Please! Everybody stop telling each other to shut up!

Norma Gordon Now you're telling us aw tae shut up, Mum.

Irene Gordon I just want us to have a nice family Christmas. Is that too much to ask?

The phone rings. No one moves to answer it.

Fine. I'll get it then, will I? Of course. You must all be shattered from your strenuous inactivity. At least your father's got an excuse. Have you had strokes? Not you, Robert.

She answers the phone.

Hello – Stewarton 482677.

Oh Trevor! Happy Christmas, son. How are you?

Well, that's good. And you've got somewhere to stay?

Em, he's fine aye. Enjoying his first proper Christmas – the wee angel . . . No, I can't lie to you, Trevor – I'm a wee bit worried about him, he's got an awful cough and I think he's shedding his feathers.

But try not to worry – we're all looking after him.

I will, aye.

I promise.

Wee Gordon's fine. His Uncle Robert's here to see him.

Oh, we're all getting on famously, it's like the Middle East peace process. Do you want a wee word with your brother?

I'll put him on. Cheerio, love, we're all missing you.

Rab takes the phone.

Rab McGuire Awright, wee broseph. Happy Christmas! How are your jingle-balls hanging?

I'm excellenty, aye.

Em she's fine, aye, I've no spoken to her today yet but I'm sure she's fine. You heard fae the folks again aye?

They'll just be skeeching down the slopes gieing it laldy.

Eh, aye – does it dae that?

To the rest:

He wants it on speakerphone.

Irene Gordon Oh really – how exciting. I love the speakerphone. Now how do you do it . . .?

She fiddles with the phone without much success. Eventually Norma takes over and puts it on.

Trevor Hello – is it working?

Everyone Yes.

Trevor Hello.

Everyone Hello.

Trevor Is Norma there?

Norma Gordon Uh-huh, I'm here.

Trevor I got the job.

There is mass jubilation. Norma and Rab are more muted and forced than the others.

Norma Gordon That's brilliant, Trevor.

Trevor Norma – will you marry me?

She looks stunned – there is a palpable atmosphere of expectation. She takes him off the speakerphone.

Norma Gordon Are you serious? Why did you think that was a good idea?
    Romantic? Oh aye, it was like a weekend in Florence, Trevor.

Listens. She is aware everyone is watching her.

Right, fine. Shut up. Alright. Yes. I will.

Irene Gordon Oh, what brilliant news. Barry – get the champagne.

Barry Gordon Champagne?

Irene Gordon You know – the cava.

Barry exits. Norma is still listening on the phone.

Norma Gordon Listen, I need to go, Trevor. I'll speak to you later.

Listens.

Yes, I said yes.

Listens.

He's fine – he's a chicken, chickens can't cough!

She hangs up. It is clear all is not well.

Irene Gordon Oh Norma – I'm so happy for you.

She hugs her.

This really is the best news.

Norma Gordon Yeah, brilliant.

Barry returns with champagne and glasses. They open the champagne and pour glasses. There is a general air of delight and chatter among all but Norma.

Norma Gordon I'll be back in a minute.

She exits. Lights on in the bathroom. Sits on the toilet composing her thoughts.

Irene Gordon Well, I better get the roasties on.

Rab McGuire I'll give you a hand.

Irene Gordon Not at all – you sit there and enjoy yourself.

She leaves. The atmosphere is incredibly awkward. Rab is clearly not enjoying himself. He breaks the silence.

Rab McGuire Sooo . . .

Irene returns.

Irene Gordon That's the roastie-toasties on. We'll eat in about an hour.

Rab McGuire Brilliant!

Norma switches the light off in the bathroom and exits.

Irene Gordon Do you like soup, Robert?

Rab McGuire Soup? Souper soup? Sure do. Who doesn't? It's like a food shake.

Irene Gordon Good, well, we've got some soup to start.

Rab McGuire Brilliant.

Irene Gordon It's cock-a-leekie.

Rab stifles a titter. Norma enters, visibly upset.

Norma Gordon Rab, can you come out here a minute?

Rab is delighted by the opportunity to escape and is up and out in almost one bound.

Rab McGuire Sure can.

Irene Gordon Are you okay, Norma?

Norma Gordon I'm fine.

Irene Gordon What's wrong?

Norma Gordon I'm fine.

Norma exits.

Irene Gordon I don't like that. I don't like that one bit. What do you think is going on?

Barry Gordon I'm sure we'll find out. That's the Queen's speech coming on.

Irene Gordon Turn it up, Gordon. Gordon!

Gordon does. 'God Save the Queen' plays. Barry stands up and salutes to aggravate his dad.

Gordon Gordon The Qu-Qu-Qu-Queen's a cu-cu-cu-cu –

Then the sudden sound of sex coming from the next room silences him. Repeated loud rhythmical banging. At first everyone attempts to ignore it but it is not ignorable. Then –

Barry Gordon Can you both hear that?

Irene Gordon No.

Barry Gordon Seriously – listen.

Irene Gordon Barry – watch the Queen.

Barry Gordon THAT'S MY SISTER. That's my sister he's doing that to.

Irene Gordon Gordon – turn the volume up.

He does so, and the National Anthem plays in increasing volume until:

The Queen Each year that passes seems to have its own character. Some leave us with a feeling of satisfaction, others are best forgotten . . .

Lights out.

Act Two

Gordon, Irene and Barry are still watching the television.

The Queen . . . We must never cease to work for a better future for ourselves and others. I wish you all, wherever you may be, a very happy Christmas.

> *'God Save the Queen' played in a calypso style rings out, signalling the end of the Queen's Christmas Day broadcast.*

Barry Gordon So are we going to talk about it?

Irene Gordon Talk about what?

Barry Gordon About Norma and –

> *Irene cuts him off.*

Irene Gordon Will you give your sister a shout – it's time for dinner. I'll just heat up the soup, can you set up the table?
Are you alright, Gordon?

Gordon Gordon Can I go to tha toilet?

Irene Gordon Take your father to the toilet first, will you?

Barry Gordon Seriously?

Irene Gordon Yes, seriously.

Barry Gordon I mean, seriously, we're all just meant to pretend that Rab and Norma weren't just –

Irene Gordon Barry, are you listening to me? Take your father to the toilet.

Barry Gordon Oh my God. This is ridiculous. Completely ridiculous. Denial much?

He gets up and pushes his father out of the door. Once they are gone, Irene sits for a moment alone, attempting to compose herself. She is on the verge of tears but holds them back. Once she has had a moment she exits to the kitchen.

Meanwhile Barry opens the bathroom door and helps his father from his wheelchair onto the toilet. He has to really struggle with him, and Gordon offers no help at all. Once Gordon is seated:

Will I just wait outside?

Gordon Gordon B-b-b-b-better give me five minuth.

Barry Gordon Nice.

Barry closes the door.
He enters the living room and returns to his position splayed out on the couch.
Irene enters.

Irene Gordon Barry! I thought you were setting up the table.

Barry Gordon I thought I was in charge of getting Dad evacuated.

Irene Gordon You can do both.

Barry Gordon Right, fine.

Irene Gordon And where's your sister?

Barry Gordon Now you want to talk about it?

Irene Gordon You were meant to be calling her and Robert. Are they coming?

Barry Gordon As her brother I find that an awkward question to answer but it certainly sounded like it, didn't it?

Irene shoots him an unimpressed glare, opens the door and shouts.

Irene Gordon NORMA! NORMA! It's time for dinner.

Meanwhile Gordon stands up and stretches in the toilet. He lights the joint and smokes it.
    Meanwhile:

And where's your father?

Barry Gordon Toilet.

Irene Gordon Did you just leave him there?

Barry Gordon He wanted me to.

Irene Gordon Do I need to do everything?

Barry Gordon No, I'll go and get him, sorry.

Irene Gordon No. You set up the table and then set it. I'll get him.

She exits. Barry starts to set up the table.
    Meanwhile, in the bathroom, Gordon lights the joint and smokes it.
    Irene knocks on the door and calls.

Gordon? Are you ready yet?

Gordon panics. He attempts to clear the smoke by inhaling deeply and waving his hands about.

Gordon Gordon Em. No. No yet. Em. I'm still shitting. I-I-I-I'm thtill thitting.

Irene Gordon Lovely. Okay. How long will you be?

Gordon Gordon Em – a few minutes.

Irene Gordon Are you alright?

Gordon Gordon Uh-huh. Em. Juth a bit conthipated.

Irene Gordon Well, don't try too hard, that can't be good for you.

Meanwhile Norma enters, looking a bit sheepish. She has sex hair. Barry ignores her for a bit before:

Barry Gordon Where's Rab?

Norma Gordon Looking after Wee Gordon.

Barry Gordon Is that what the kids are calling it now?

Norma Gordon What's that supposed to mean?

Barry Gordon What do you think?

Norma realises.

Thin walls. You know we've got thin walls.

Norma Gordon Oh my God. No. You don't understand.

Barry Gordon 'I've been on the internet.'

Norma Gordon No! Oh God, Barry! It isn't what you think! I swear.

Barry Gordon I'm setting the table.

Norma Gordon I swear.

Irene enters.

Irene Gordon There you are. Is little Gordon alright?

Norma Gordon Em. Fine. Em. Mum . . .

Rab enters. He too has sex hair.

Rab McGuire Awright, Gordons, what have I missed? Was the Queen good? God bless her.

Barry Gordon The soundtrack was distressing.

Rab McGuire Oh aye? How so?

Irene Gordon We're just about to eat. Could you give Norma a hand setting the table, Robert?

Rab McGuire Aye, no worries.

Irene Gordon Barry – go and get your father.

Barry Gordon Fine.

He exits. Rab and Norma set the table while Irene goes to the kitchen to collect the soup. Once they are alone:

Norma Gordon Oh my fucking actual God, Rab.

Rab McGuire I know. That's was awright, wint it?

Norma Gordon NO! They heard.

Rab McGuire What?

Norma Gordon EVERYTHING! *They heard everything, Rab!*

Rab McGuire No.

Norma Gordon Aye.

Rab McGuire No.

Norma Gordon Aye.

Rab McGuire No.
Oh.
Fuck.
Fuck, man.
Fuck.

Norma Gordon Uh-huh.

Rab McGuire Right. Well. I'm away then, I'm just going to grab my jacket.

He makes to leave. Norma grabs his arm.

Norma Gordon You're going nowhere.

Rab McGuire I know – chill, I was joking, man.

Norma Gordon Well, don't. We're fucked. Totally, totally fucked.

Rab McGuire What have they said?

Norma Gordon My mum's said nothing but Barry telt me.

Rab McGuire Oh Christ, Barry, man.

Norma Gordon And what about My mum and dad? And Trevor?

Rab McGuire Seriously – fuck Trevor, man. *I love you.*

Irene enters, and they quickly silence.
    Meanwhile: Barry knocks on the door.

Barry Gordon Dad – you done?

Gordon unlocks it.

Jeeso, it reeks of weed.

He helps his father off the toilet and into the wheelchair. He switches off the light and closes the door.
    Meanwhile:

Norma Gordon Em . . . Mum . . . I need to talk to you about Trevor.

Irene Gordon Oh yes?

Norma Gordon Listen – about me and Trevor . . .

Irene Gordon Not just now, Norma.

Norma Gordon But . . . em . . . it's quite important . . .

Irene Gordon Not just now it isn't.

Norma Gordon Mum . . .

Irene Gordon Robert, could you go and check on Wee Gordon for me? Just make sure he's down alright?

Rab McGuire Aye, no bother.

He exits.

Irene Gordon Norma – I don't ask for much from any of you. I just want us all to sit down together as a family and enjoy the dinner which I've spent all day preparing and all week organising and all month looking forward to. I don't think that's too much to ask, is it?
Is it?

Norma Gordon No.

Irene Gordon I don't want any drama.

Norma Gordon No, but . . .

Irene Gordon NO BUTS.

Norma Gordon No, but Mum . . .

Irene Gordon WHAT?

Norma Gordon Mum . . . I really need to talk to you . . .

Irene Gordon No, Norma. Not just now. We're just about to have our dinner.

Norma Gordon Mum, please . . .

Irene Gordon You and your brother and your father . . . it's like you're all a different species. I don't understand any of you. At all. I just want my family and food to eat and a roof over my head. I don't know what it is you all want, but I hope you find it, Norma . . .

Norma Gordon Mum . . .

Irene Gordon Because you just look at your father if you want to see what life's like when you don't.

Norma Gordon Mum. I'm sorry, Mum. I'm sorry.

Irene ignores her and exits. Barry enters with Gordon, followed by Rab. Irene puts the light on and enters the downstairs toilet. She closes the door behind her, smells the weed and storms back out.

Rab McGuire Right. So . . . everyone's cool, let's Christmas!

Gordon *and* **Barry** SHUT UP, RAB!

Rab McGuire Fine. Jeeso.

Irene storms in. Furious.

Irene Gordon BARRY GORDON! That is the final straw.

Barry Gordon What?

Irene Gordon Go and smell the toilet.

Norma Gordon Mum!

Barry Gordon What?

Irene Gordon It stinks like a Dutch labour exchange in there.

Barry looks at Gordon.

Barry, I love you but I cannot keep letting you waste yourself.

Barry Gordon I'm not wasting myself.

Irene Gordon What kind of mother would I be to you if I just turned a blind eye and let you keep smoking that stuff?

Barry Gordon I haven't been!

Irene Gordon I can't believe you are lying right to my face.

Barry Gordon I'm not. I only had that joint earlier. I haven't been smoking any since. And anyway – it's no different to drinking alcohol.

Irene Gordon And if you spent all day every day drinking and playing on your computer I'd have a problem with that too. You'd be an alcoholic.

Barry Gordon But I don't and I'm not.

Irene Gordon No, you're a potaholic.

Barry Gordon I'm not a potaholic. I just smoke a little weed. It's fine.

Irene Gordon It's my house and I'm saying no more.

Barry Gordon Fine. Right. I hear you.

Irene Gordon No, it isn't fine. I told you this afternoon. I warned you.

Barry Gordon But I didn't.

Irene Gordon I'M NOT STUPID! I know what pot smells like.

Barry Gordon IT WASN'T ME.

Irene Gordon Then who was it?

Barry gives Gordon the opportunity to confess. He doesn't.

Barry Gordon It was Dad.

Irene Gordon Your dad's had a stroke. Gordon?

Gordon Gordon Eh . . . it . . . w-w-w-w-wisnae me.

Barry Gordon Fuck you, you lying old bastard.

Irene Gordon BARRY! I'd like you to leave.

Barry Gordon You're believing him?

Irene Gordon Gordon?

He puts on a face like he's sorry it's come to this, but can't lie for his son.

58

Barry Gordon I can't believe you're believing him over me.

Irene Gordon I wish I didn't. I wish I didn't think you were a liar, Barry. But you keep lying.

Barry Gordon Norma's the one who got pregnant. Dad's the one who left you for some daft lassy. Why am I getting all this shit?

Gordon Gordon Watch your mouth, son.

Barry Gordon Oh, is this you giving me some much needed parental authority? A strong male role model? Too late. About twenty-two years too late.

Gordon Gordon Don't push me.

Barry Gordon If I don't push you how will you get to the toilet?

Gordon suddenly grabs Barry with his right arm and pulls him close to him. They face off, Gordon breathing heavily and threateningly right in Barry's face.

Irene Gordon What are you doing, Gordon?

Rab McGuire Eh . . . guys . . .

Gordon releases him.

Barry Gordon He's gone mental.

Norma Gordon Barry – he's had a stroke.

Barry Gordon You've all gone mental.

Irene Gordon I'm serious, Barry – just leave.

Barry Gordon He's a psycho, she's fucking her son's uncle and you're in denial.

Rab McGuire Barry, man . . .

Irene Gordon Barry, please . . .

Barry Gordon Fine.

He leaves.

Norma Gordon Barry, wait. Mum?

Gordon Gordon Let him go.

Norma Gordon NO! It isn't up to you any more.

Irene Gordon Norma.

Norma Gordon What? It isn't. He left.

Irene Gordon He's still your father.

Norma Gordon I know, but he left us all. It wasn't just you he left.

Irene Gordon Norma, please.

Norma Gordon Well it's true, in'tit? He left us all.

Irene Gordon He loves you both.

Gordon Gordon Ahm still here.

Norma Gordon If he loved us so much he wouldn't have been fucking Amber Pearce, would he? She was two years above me in school.

Irene Gordon Norma, please.

Norma Gordon And she's pure fat!

Irene Gordon Norma!

Norma Gordon Sometimes you need to talk about things, Mum. Sometimes sticking your fingers in your ears and going nah-nah-nah isn't the best policy.

Irene Gordon I just want us to have a nice Christmas dinner.

Norma Gordon What about Barry? What about him? Will it be a nice Christmas dinner if you're worrying about Barry?

Irene Gordon I worry about him even when he's here.

Norma Gordon Mum, you know what I mean. He's being an idiot, but he's our idiot. We should all be here for Christmas.

Rab McGuire Em . . . listen, maybe I should –

Irene Gordon Trevor should be here too.

Norma Gordon I need to talk to you about Trevor.

Irene Gordon No, you don't. You think I didn't get the idea when I heard you and Robert, who's your brother-in-law in all but name. You nearly came though the wall.

Rab McGuire Em . . .

Norma Gordon I'm sorry, Mum.

Irene Gordon Sorry's easy said, Norma. You've got Wee Gordon to think about. He's Trevor's son.

Norma Gordon Trevor and me . . . Mum, we're not in love. We never were.

Irene Gordon So? So? You young people. You think love is like a lottery win. Something that suddenly just happens to you and changes everything. Well it isn't, Norma.

Rab McGuire Em . . . listen, will I . . .

Irene Gordon Love is like savings. It's an investment you make. It's more about family than it is about sex.

Rab McGuire Listen, I'm just going to . . .

Norma Gordon Mum, you're giving me a beamer.

Irene Gordon Grow up, Norma. You think I wanted to hear my daughter, my wee girl, my only wee girl rutting through the wall?

Rab McGuire Aye, listen, I'll just look in on the wee man.

He exits.

Norma Gordon Mum . . .

Irene Gordon Trevor is the baby's father. You need to try and make it work. For Gordon.

Norma Gordon I love Rab.

Irene Gordon Norma. Robert's Trevor's brother. He's Gordon's uncle. It can't happen.

Norma Gordon It has happened.

Irene Gordon It isn't a good idea.

Norma Gordon So? What does being a good idea have to do with it? I love him and he loves me. And the other kind of love. The one you're talking about. Well, that might be fine for you, Mum, but I don't want a love that means taking my husband back after he's made a show of me in front of the whole of Stewarton. I don't think that is love, Mum. I think that's stupidity.

Irene Gordon Norma.

Norma Gordon What? You can tell me what you think's wrong with me but I can't tell you what I think is wrong with you? Well that's just shite, Mum.

Gordon Gordon Norma . . .

Irene Gordon I haven't taken your father back. I'm looking after him. He sleeps downstairs.

Norma Gordon Och aye. For how long though, Mum? How long until you are back together? It's not like you're going to meet anyone else with him here all the time.

Gordon Gordon Norma . . .

Irene Gordon Norma, I don't want to meet anyone else.

Norma Gordon Exactly. He's got you right where he wants you.

Irene Gordon Norma – this is none of your business.

Norma Gordon But it is. He made it my business when he started messing around with a girl I went to school with. Do you know how embarrassing that is?

Irene Gordon YES. OF COURSE I DO.

Gordon Gordon I'm sorry . . .

Norma Gordon But you still took him back.

Irene Gordon He had a stroke, Norma. Who else was going to look after him?

Norma Gordon What about Amber?

Irene Gordon She's a wee lassy.

Norma Gordon Exactly! That's his problem. He made his bed. Let him lie in it.

Irene Gordon No. Don't you see, Norma? You talk about love like it's something you understand. But you don't understand at all. Because that's what love is.

Norma Gordon Well, I don't want any part in that love.

Irene Gordon 'That love' – you say that like there's any other. It's the only love there is. The other stuff is just hormonal teenage nonsense –

Norma Gordon I'm a mother! I'm not a kid!

Irene Gordon – but it goes both ways, Norma. You need someone there for you too.

Norma Gordon You just don't understand.

Irene Gordon Trevor proposes one minute and the next you're in bed with his brother? Norma, it's like a *Daily Record* headline.

Norma Gordon NO. It isn't like that. It isn't like that.

Irene Gordon Oh Norma. Do what you like. You always do.

Norma Gordon That's not true.

Irene Gordon That thing you're talking about. That love. It's like a flick knife on a school trip, Norma. It's only fun for the person holding it. Everyone else can see it's dangerous and pointless and stupid and destructive.

Norma Gordon Love *is* selfish.

Irene Gordon What do you know about it? Love isn't selfish. It's generous.

Norma Gordon Well, you're certainly giving it away.

Gordon Gordon NORMA!

Irene Gordon Oh Norma, don't. Please. Please don't.

Norma Gordon Right. Well, if Barry isn't staying then I'm not either.

Irene Gordon Where are you going?

Norma Gordon I'm going to Rab's and we're taking grotbags with us.

Irene Gordon NO, YOU ARE NOT!

Norma Gordon He's my son.

Irene Gordon Norma, please.

Norma Gordon No, if you think so little of me. If you think I'm just some daft wee lassy.

Irene Gordon You are.

Norma Gordon Well I hope you're happy.

Gordon Gordon Norma. Love.

Norma Gordon Twice you've managed to tear our family apart. We're in quarters now.

Gordon Gordon Norma.

Norma Gordon I hope you're happy.

Norma opens the door and shouts.

RAB! Get together Wee Gordon's things! We're going.

Irene Gordon I'm thinking of Wee Gordon. Your brother has got a problem.

Norma Gordon Hello? This whole family has got problems!

Irene Gordon I'm thinking of Gordon.

Gordon Gordon Wait. W-w-w-wait.

Norma Gordon What?

Gordon Gordon I-I-I-Irene. It, em, it was me who smoked the joint.

Irene Gordon What?

Gordon Gordon S-s-s-s-sorry.

Furious silence.

Irene Gordon If you weren't ill I would slap you, so help me, Gordon.

Gordon Gordon I'm sorry. Ith Christmas. I th-th-thought that it would b-b-b-be better Barry – in th-th-the circumstances.

Irene Gordon I can't even look at you.

She turns him around to face the wall.

Gordon Gordon Irene. Irene, pleath.

Rab enters. He and Gordon stare at each other for a moment, then –

Rab McGuire What did you shout, Norma?

Irene Gordon I'm sorry, Norma.

Norma Gordon I'm sorry too.

Irene Gordon We need to find your brother.

Norma Gordon I'll call him.

She gets out her mobile.

Rab McGuire Eh . . . so what have I missed?

Norma Gordon My dad's an arsehole.

Rab McGuire Right. Em, are you alright there, Mr Gordon?

Gordon Gordon Turn me round.

Rab goes to do so. Irene stops him.

Irene Gordon Leave him.

Rab McGuire Em. Right.

Norma Gordon It's going to his voicemail.
Barry, call me back, or just come home. It's fine. We know it was Dad. I'm sorry. Please just come home.

Irene takes the phone.

Irene Gordon Barry, please. I'm so sorry. Just come home. Please.

She hangs up.

Rab McGuire Em . . . sorry . . . I don't want to . . . eh . . . but can anyone else smell burning?

Irene Gordon THE FOOD!

She rushes off to the kitchen.

Rab McGuire What's going on?

Gordon Gordon Turn me around.

Rab looks to Norma.

Norma Gordon Don't.

Rab McGuire What have I missed?

Norma Gordon Dad was smoking weed in the toilet.

Rab McGuire Oh right. Really?

Gordon Gordon Turn me around.

Rab McGuire And did he say . . . I mean how did he . . . em . . . So he just rolled himself a joint and smoked it ay?

Norma Gordon Uh-huh.

Rab McGuire Right.

Irene enters. She throws a charred roast potato at Gordon's head and exits. Norma goes after her.

Norma Gordon Mum . . .

Rab McGuire Em. Cheers for no ratting me out, Mr G.

Gordon Gordon Turn me around.

Rab McGuire Em . . . I'd like to. I mean, you know I'd like to. If it was up to me. I mean. If it was up to me you know I would, but . . . em . . .

Gordon Gordon What have I done?

Rab McGuire Yeah. Mental.

Gordon Gordon What am I going to do?

Rab goes to face Gordon.

Just turn me around, son.

He does it with an air of resignation.

I have fucked everything up.

Rab McGuire Och you had a wee toke and you let Barry take the blame. No the end of the world is it? I think it's more me and Norma that's got tempers fraying. You know. Em. Sorry.

Gordon Gordon You love her?

Rab McGuire Aye.

Gordon Gordon But really? For ever? Her and the wean?

Rab McGuire For real. For ever. Her and the wean.

Gordon Gordon You'll need to.
     What's your dad like?

Rab McGuire Em. My dad? You've met him. He's alright. He's just a dad, you know? Pringle sweaters, specs, Laguna. Dad stuff.

Gordon Gordon But what's he like?

Rab McGuire Aye, I'd say he's a good guy, aye.

Gordon Gordon I never wanted to be a dad, son. I fucking hated it. I hated using a johnny but you see – So me and Irene used to do it like Irish peasants because she wouldn't use the pill.

Rab McGuire Are you sure you want to tell me this?

Gordon Gordon So we just used to do it bareback. I'd just pull out and come on her stomach, you know.

Rab McGuire Right.

Gordon Gordon I fucking hated using a johnny, but oh Christ, if I'd only known . . .

Rab McGuire This is a bit . . .

Gordon Gordon So Barry was an accident. Then we had to get married. That was what it was like in they days. And once we were married we barely did it again. Maybe once or twice before Norma.

Rab McGuire Listen, Mr G. This is all a wee bit . . .

Gordon Gordon And then I was a family man. And I love my kids. Don't get me wrong. I fucking love them, but I always had this niggling sense of being trapped by them and Irene. Like I was a prisoner or something.

Rab McGuire I'm sure everyone feels like that. Don't they?

Gordon Gordon No. Just useless, selfish bastards like me.

You know about me losing my job?

Rab McGuire Aye.

Gordon Gordon Course you do. Wee June is your Michelle's mum.

Rab McGuire Em. Aye. To be honest, man, every cunt in Stewarton knows about that.

Gordon Gordon Those are not the actions of a committed family man.

Rab McGuire No.

Gordon Gordon But Irene stood by me. She knew what I'd done, messed around with a pupil, and she stood by me. She's like a fucking lioness, that woman.

Rab McGuire Aye, she's something.

Gordon Gordon After I lost my job I was just . . . I don't know . . . depression they'd call it now. Best part of twenty years. And then when Barry started going out with Michelle it kicked up all the shit again. With Irene. And me. And them. And I just. I don't know. I snapped. Something just tore inside me and I walked out. But I didn't mean to hurt them. I didn't. Because I fucking love them.

Rab McGuire Do you know anything about circus monkeys?

Gordon Gordon What?

Rab McGuire Circus monkeys, right – a circus monkey is only good for about seven or eight years of work. That's aw they can cope wi. I mean, they're fine for that long but then. Poof. They decide tae bin it. And when the decision's made the decision's made.

And that can happen at any point – hanging aboot wi the other monkeys, in the middle of a show – no one ever knows when exactly a monkey suddenly says to himself, 'Right – fuck this.'

But when he does, right, he just stops in the middle of whatever it was he was doing.

Gordon Gordon Circus monkeys? Are you retarded, son?

Rab McGuire So he stops and he waves his arms slowly in a criss-cross above his head.

Rab demonstrates.

Like he's surrendering or something. And then he stops. And then he goes fucking mental.

Something inside him snaps – all those years of daft wee hats and tiny bicycles or whatever and all the dancing for the crowds, performing and travelling and living in a cage – all of it just builds up in him and the minute he's done, the minute he says to himself, 'Right, I am fucking sick of this fucking shit, man,' all his years of fucking bitterness and resentment and whatever just wells up and he goes radge. He fucking launches himself at whatever cunt's nearest.

And the cunt who gets it, more often than not, is the clown on stage with him. Fucking Coco or Bozo or whoever.

Monkeys are pure vicious, man, vicious – they're right wee bastards when they want to be and they're hard as fuck. There's biting and scratching and eye-gouging and aw the dirty shit. And they scream like fuck an aw.

Rab does a violent monkey scream.

So they tear the face off Bozo. I mean they literally tear the fucking face right off him.

And you know the worst thing, man? About the circus monkeys?

The other clowns, they just fucking leave you to it. Brutal in'tit? When a monkey goes mental none of the other clowns will try and help you. Fucking clowns, man. Selfish cunts.

Gordon stands up.

No way! No way!

Gordon Gordon Uh-huh.

Rab McGuire And this isnae a Lazarus thing, no?

Gordon Gordon No.

Rab McGuire Fuck me.

He sits back down.

Gordon Gordon So what am I meant to do now? Tell me that. What am I meant to do now?

Norma enters.

Norma Gordon Turn him back to the wall and ignore him.

Rab McGuire Em, I can't do that, man. How's your mum?

Norma Gordon She's in bits. The dinner's fucked.

Rab McGuire Em. Do you want me to go and get a carry-out?

Norma Gordon Eh . . . I don't know. I suppose so.

Rab McGuire Right. What's everyone want?

Norma Gordon My mum wants a vegetable stir fry with cashew nuts – it's not on the menu but if you ask they'll do it for you. Barry wants kung po chicken and I want lemon chicken. And we like fried rice not boiled.

Rab McGuire What about you, Mr G?

Norma Gordon Don't get him anything. He doesn't deserve anything.

Gordon Gordon Norma.

Norma Gordon Don't.

Gordon Gordon I'm sorry.

Norma Gordon Get him chicken curry with boiled rice.

Gordon Gordon I don't like . . .

Norma Gordon I know you don't.

Rab McGuire Right. I'll be back in a minute.

Norma Gordon See if you can find Barry.

Rab McGuire Right. Aye.

Norma Gordon Thanks, Rab.

She kisses him before returning to the kitchen to see her mum.

Rab McGuire You need to tell them.

Gordon Gordon It's Christmas.
Aye. I know.
I just wanted a second chance, you know . . . I saw what I'd done. To them all. And not just leaving them then. And Amber. And all that. Everything. Not being

the man that this family deserved. And I just wanted a second chance.

Rab McGuire Well . . . third time's the charm.

Gordon Gordon I even fucked my second chance.

Rab McGuire If it's any consolation – it wisnae exactly going to work out over the long term anyway. Even if you hadn't – I mean, were you really planning to pretend you'd hud a stroke for the rest of your life?

Gordon Gordon I thought I would just . . . get better.

Rab McGuire The eternal optimism of the human condition. That might be your downfall and your salvation though but.

Barry enters.

Gordon Gordon Barry. I'm sorry, Barry. I'm sorry.

Rab McGuire Awright, man.

Barry Gordon I hate you both.

Rab McGuire Fair enough, man. I'm going to the Chinese. Kung po chicken is it?

Barry Gordon What happened to dinner?

Rab McGuire Em, it's a wee bit ruined.

Barry Gordon That's this family all over. Wee Trevor has escaped. He doesn't look ill though, I'd say he looked quite spry when I saw him running down the chooky brae. Ironically.

Gordon Gordon Barry.

He stands up.

I'm sorry Barry. I didn't have a stroke.
   I've got angina.

Barry Gordon I know.

Gordon Gordon What?

Barry Gordon I know that.

Gordon Gordon How?

Barry Gordon It was fucking obvious. I kept expecting Mum or Norma to realise too.

Gordon Gordon But you just let me . . .

Barry Gordon I thought you'd come to your senses. Once you saw that you were only welcome through pity. That we'd moved on. That the only place for you here now was downstairs on the sofa bed.

Gordon Gordon That's better than nothing – it's better than being in that wee flat in Dunlop Street.
   You didn't tell them. Before. When I let you take the blame for . . . You didn't tell them.

Barry Gordon I know. I was waiting for you to do the right thing. Waiting for the tiny shred of decency that I had assumed must be in there somewhere to come out. I was giving you a chance, right up till the door closed behind me.
   And then I was just a bit surprised, really. You never stopped me.
   So I went for a walk. Thought about what I've become if Mum believed you over me.

Gordon Gordon Barry, I'm sorry.

Barry Gordon Uh-huh, sure, don't be. I've had a Christmas epiphany. I have been a complete dick.
   MUM! NORMA!

They rush through. They are both so excited to see Barry that neither of them immediately notices Gordon's Lazarus-like recovery.

Irene Gordon BARRY!

Norma Gordon You're back!

Irene grabs hold of Barry and squeezes him within an inch of his life.

Barry Gordon Alright, Mum.

Irene Gordon I'm really sorry.

Barry Gordon It's fine. I've been a dick.

Irene Gordon Oh Barry, I'm sorry.

Norma Gordon Hold on.

She stares at Gordon.

Mum, Dad's standing. He's standing up.

Irene Gordon Well, that puts paid to the concept of karma.

Norma Gordon That's amazing, though. It's a Christmas miracle.

Barry Gordon Isn't it?

Gordon Gordon Norma . . . Irene . . . I've got something I need to tell you.

Norma Gordon You even sound better.

Gordon Gordon I've got some good news and some bad news . . .

Irene Gordon No. This is a joke. No.

Norma Gordon What? What is it?

Irene Gordon There's nothing wrong with him. There was never anything wrong with him.

Gordon Gordon I've got angina.

Norma Gordon No way.

Gordon Gordon I've got angina.

Irene slaps him as hard as she can. He absorbs it stoically.

I realised I'd made a mistake.

Irene Gordon A mistake? Which one? Gordon, every single decision you have ever made has been a mistake.

Gordon Gordon I just thought maybe I could win you all back.

Irene Gordon Win us back? You are a complete bastard.

To everyone else:

I'm sorry for my language.

Barry Gordon It's fine.

Norma Gordon Dad? I can't believe it. I can't believe it.

Gordon Gordon I'm sorry, Norma.

Norma Gordon What the eff? I mean, really, what the eff? Are you a psychopath or something?

Gordon Gordon I'm just a man who's made some mistakes and realised too late how lucky he is. I'm just a man who loves his family.

Barry Gordon Like Charles Manson.

Gordon Gordon I'll go.

Barry Gordon Finally.

Irene Gordon Tomorrow.

Norma Gordon What?

Irene Gordon He'll go tomorrow. It's Christmas Day.

Barry Gordon Mum?

Irene Gordon This is what it's like to be a family. You make do and make the best of things and you stay together.

Gordon Gordon Irene, I can't tell you how . . .

Irene Gordon I think it might be better if you said as little as possible now, Gordon.

Norma Gordon Mum, you cannae be serious.

Irene Gordon It's like I've been trying to explain to you, Norma. Blood ties and commitment are what make families. And they endure.

Norma Gordon Mum . . .

Irene Gordon It's like climbing a mountain. The journey is important but you do it for the summit. And if you keep giving up at the start you'll never reach it.

Norma Gordon You've got to climb the mountain you want to see the summit of, though.

Irene Gordon Robert, would you go down to the Oriental Palace and pick us up some food?

Rab McGuire No bother. Vegetable stir fry with cashew nuts, kung po chicken, lemon chicken, a chicken curry and boiled rice, and fried for everyone else?

Irene Gordon Who's the chicken curry and boiled rice for?

Rab McGuire Mr Gordon.

Irene Gordon No. Get him duck in plumb sauce and fried rice for everybody.

Rab McGuire Right. No bother.

He makes to leave. Stops.

Mrs Gordon. Barry. Mr Gordon. I just want to say something.

Barry Gordon Oh God.

Rab McGuire I am in love with Norma. I know how it must look from the outside but I am in love with her and have been for years. It's just taken till recently for me to realise it. I love her and I love the wee man. I'm not going anywhere so . . . I just thought I should let you know.

Barry Gordon I'll let Trevor know.

Rab McGuire Trevor's my brother and I love him too, and I hope he forgives me, obviously.
But . . .
I promise you all that I will do right by Norma.
And, em. That's it.

He exits. The Gordon family stand around for a moment, looking at each other. Eventually Irene, Norma and Barry sit down and put on the TV. Gordon watches them for a minute then makes to sit down too.

Irene Gordon In the wheelchair.

He sits in the wheelchair.

Barry Gordon We haven't even done the presents yet.

Irene Gordon Let's wait until Rab's back.

Sound of a cockerel crowing.

The End.